Saturday Morning CEO:

How two hours a week will guarantee your business and personal success in any economy.

W. Denis Nurmela

Saturday Morning CEO Publishing

Published by Saturday Morning CEO Publishing Department

Menifee, California

Warning – Disclaimer:

The purpose of this book is to educate and entertain. The author or publisher does not guarantee that anyone following the techniques, suggestions, tips, ideas, or strategies will become successful. The author and publisher shall have neither liability or responsibility to anyone with respect to any loss or damage caused, or alleged to be caused, directly or indirectly by the information contained in this book.

ISBN:1468068776
ISBN-13:978-1468068771

www.SaturdayMorningCEO.com

DEDICATION

This book is the culmination of knowledge gained in the trenches of everyday life in the business world, as well as many years of graduate and post-graduate business degree schooling. During these years my lovely wife, Cynthia, has been there urging me on, putting up with my crazy ideas, allowing me to study, and praying for success during times of challenge.

I dedicate this book to my wife, Cynthia, and our 6 wonderful children that we are blessed with: Sandy, David, Sarah, Michael, Daniel, and Aaron.

Table of Contents

ACKNOWLEDGMENTS 8

1 Why Saturday Morning? 11

   Accountability 13

   Preparation 15

   Idea Filter 16

   Measure Progress 19

   Study and Compare 20

   Press Box View 22

2 Peak Energy Type 27

3 Structure of Your 2 Hours 32

   Focus 33

   Agenda 35

      Checklist 38

      Measurable 40

      Mentor Trackable 42

   Open/Close Routine 43

   Daily Journaling with Purpose 46

   Habit Forming / Trusted System 47

4 Agenda Item: Life Balance 52

   Prioritize 53

   Quick Rating 56

   Focus on Strengths 58

5 Agenda Item: Mission/Vision.. 63

    Source of Passion 65

    Alignment & Focus 67

    Look Through Different Lenses 69

6 Agenda Item: Goals... 74

    Personal/Family... 75

    Business... 76

7 Agenda Item: Personal SWOT 80

    Opportunities / Threats.. 82

8 Agenda Item: Innovations 86

    Core Competency Improvements 87

    Family Innovations.. 88

9 Agenda Item: Action Plan 92

    Task Management & Execution 92

10 Agenda Item: Evaluation 97

    Take-Aways.. 97

    Constraint Management.. 98

    Next Week's Agenda... 100

11 Agenda Item: "Hammock Time".................................... 103

12 Read This First 106

ABOUT THE AUTHOR 111

ACKNOWLEDGMENTS

It is difficult to claim that any single idea in this book is original. Rather, it is a compilation of the knowledge gained from books, papers, studies, business experiences, personal associations, family relationships, friendships, faith experiences, and conversations with others which has shaped this manuscript. A few individuals, however, need to be acknowledged as special contributors to the culmination of ideas in my biological database, and in the execution of this book.

My Parents, Wayne & Toni; Brother, Scott, and Sister, Christy: helped me develop My worldview about life, business & the pursuit of happiness.

God: My relationship with God has brought strength and comfort through every challenge, joy, sorrow, and passion in life's journey here on earth.

Bentley J. Tolk: My friend and 'brother' who, with his family, have been examples of honesty, spirituality, friendship, family, loyalty, ethics and love.

Dave Paton: My longtime business associate and dearest friend, who has served as a governing board member of many of my business ventures, and has shared with me a "full speed ahead" attitude toward overcoming challenges and taking advantage of opportunities.

Gary Lockwood: My business mentor and friend. He helped me see life from a different set of lenses. Now I make decisions from the "press box."

Craig Duswalt: Founder of the RockStar System for Success. Craig motivated me to get this book done, and he also encouraged me to make music a priority in my life, which has opened new sources of passion to me.

Giants of motivation and advice who have inspired and guided my inner-most passions in life through their spoken and written words: Zig Ziglar, Og Mandino, Earl Nightingale, Dale Carnegie, Stephen Covey, Tony Robbins, William H. Danforth, Brian Tracy, Denis Waitley, Bill Cosby, Napoleon Hill, Michael E. Gerber, Russell H. Conwell &Eli M. Goldratt.

My greatest strength and motivation has come from anyone who said things like, "That is impossible,"or "It has never been done before." They might as well have said, "I double-dog dare you!"

CHAPTER ONE

"Until we can manage time, we can manage nothing else."
Peter F. Drucker

1 Why Saturday Morning?

How often do you feel like you are running endless circles on a hamster wheel, seeming to go nowherevery quickly? Go ahead, no one is looking…nod your head if you have ever felt this way.

Most people don't realize that even as the CEO of a company, or as an entrepreneurial rising star,it's just as easy to get caught in the repetitive cycles of life and begin to lose focus on yourgoals and direction, as it is for anyone else on this big blue ball we call earth.

The hamster wheel of life becomes very addicting.Wheneverwe find that things seem to be working we just keep running on it, trying to run faster to accomplish more. No worries about that little squeak starting up on the wheel. It is probably nothing…just ignore it and run faster.

I've had the experience of being on many a hamster wheel, and have helped coach and mentor others who were running on their own wheels. I have been a business owner since I was nine years old. I have seen my share of poorly maintained wheels, and have seen some crash to the ground.

I've found that it doesn't matter if your hamster wheel is made of cardboard or solid gold; they all need to have some quality,regularly-scheduled preventive maintenance done, and at times we need to abandon our beloved old wheel for a new one.

If you haven't stopped nodding your head in agreement, then you can do so now-because we are going to start talking about how to fix the eternal turning of the squeaky wheel.

Once a week, it is imperative thatyou have a one-on-one strategic planning meeting with yourself to keep your focus, steady your balance onlife, and re-energize your passions.

Saturday mornings can be a perfect timefor this personal planning meeting. It is usually free from work responsibilities, and when you rise earlier than everyone else you are not cutting into your social time with family and friends.

While there are variations in our peak energy types, we all need to set up our planning meetings,even if at different times of the week (we will discuss your peak energy type in chapter 2). In this book we will call this two-hour strategic planning meeting a Saturday morning event.

In this book, some terminology will be easily recognized by CEOs who have training as master planners and strategic managers. However, this book can also be useful for new entrepreneurs and individuals who have a desire to become better organized to accomplish more in their life. So, whether you are a seasoned CEO of a large company, or a young entrepreneur, the principles and concepts of this book will work for you when you apply them.

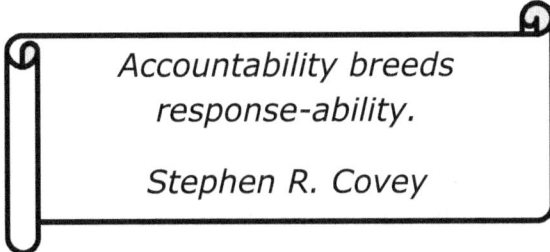

Accountability breeds response-ability.

Stephen R. Covey

When I was in my 20s I used to run 6 miles nearly every morning. It was not uncommon for me to run a 10K (6.2 mile) race in 45 minutes. I maintainedmy great shape and healthy lifestyle through the first few years of my United States Air Force service. However, they really do feed you well in the Air Force. I never knew anything about portion control, or eating just three times a day. I also had the opinion that 1 pound of cheesecake must contain the same nutrients as one pound of chicken or 1 pound of salad.

I later was married,andI was blessed with a wife who is a wonderful cook.We alsosubscribed to cable television. These factors, over time, blessed me with an extra 100 pounds of beauty to the girth of my physical frame. I've been on the Atkins diet, the see-food diet, and alkaline-based diet, and I've even purchased gym memberships occasionally.I evenusedthem! I had the best of luck losing weight when my wife and I were both following the Weight Watchers® program. However, I always seemed to quickly find whatever weight I lost in these programs.

It wasn't until I made the decision to follow my own business advice of being accountable to a mentor that I started seeing real success. I started working with Paul David, owner of Elevate Fitness Studios, one of the most sought after personal trainers in Southern California. Paul has not only become my fitness guru and mentor, but has become a very dear friend. And he is notthe kind of friend who tells you what you *want* hear;instead, he is the kind of friend who tells you what you *need* to hear.

Paul has truly cared about my personal fitness, and I have become very accountable to him. He and I share a private Facebook group page where I post pictures of the food that I eat,andhe can either make supportive comments or provide needed lessons about what needs to change regarding my eating habits.

By becoming more accountable to Paul I gained a greater understanding of how hard it is for me to be accountable to myself alone. I can think there are many areas in my life, both personal and professional, where much room exists for improvement. You might be thinking the same way right now as a result ofa missed opportunity with a customer, a failed business partnership, a missed piano recital or soccer game, or even a damaged relationship.

I can't tell you how many times I thought or even verbally said the words, "one of these days I'm going to…" Those things never seem to happen, ever. The only way to accomplish what we know we must do is to write it down, prioritize it, break it into doable tasks, calendar the tasks, and then do them.

By holding a regular meeting with yourself once a week, you will become accountable to yourself, and you will have a record of all your plans so that you can review them with your business mentor.

The more accountable we become, as the quote by Stephen Covey states at the beginning of this section, the better response we can have when opportunities arise,orwhen we are confronted with challenges. We all seem to be very determined to do what we must do. However, it is often much more difficult to remember *what* we must do; and when we do remember, we often have so many things to do that we either choose to do the easiest first, or mix up the order of importance and priority.

Preparation

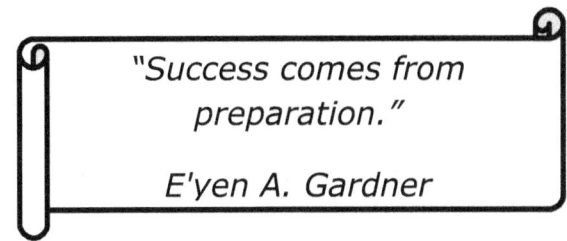

"Success comes from preparation."

E'yen A. Gardner

This weekly planning time with yourself will be one of the most important meetings that you have all week long. It is important that you **properly prepare** for this meeting. You'll be able to do so all week long as you listen to ideas from others, have thoughts and ideas of your own, keep a record of your meetings with others, the decisions you made, and the time that you spent with your family and friends.

The day before your meeting you should spend a little time reviewing the thoughts that you had during the week. You may have recorded them on a digital recorder, or kept notes from meetings you attended.Every "eureka" idea that may have transpired in your mind during the week should be captured and brought to the meeting.

Some people who keep a written calendar highlight or put an asterisk next to an event that they would like to revisit on the next agenda. There is a great book written by David Allen, called *Getting Things Done: The art of stress-free productivity,*[1] which shares a plethora of ideas on becoming organized and more efficient in accomplishing all the tasks on your plate every day.

Idea Filter

> "My ideas usually come not at my desk writing but in the midst of living."
>
> *Anais Nin*

Your weekly meeting will become the place the you consider the bucket full of ideas and suggestions that you received all week long.

---

[1] Allen, D. (2001). Getting things done: the art of stress-free productivity. New York: Viking.

Have you ever been driving down the road and had an earthshaking idea, and then somebody cuts you off and you forgot whatthe idea was? I thought so ...me too. Hassomeone ever shared a great idea with you in the middle of a conversation at a busy networking meeting, and you thought the idea was so good that there's no way you would forget it? Me,too. But, I can't remember what it was.

I used to have trouble going to sleep at night. I would toss and turn try to get comfortable, but just as I started to fall asleep, my brain would suddenly turn on, and at raging speed start-rapid firing some of the best ideas I have had all day. I'm talking world-peace ideas. They were so inspiring,and such great ideas, that I knew in my relaxed state that there wasno way I could possibly not remember them in the morning... and you know how much of it I remembered in the morning, right? Zero. I'm assuming that you have experienced the same form of inspiration followed by amnesia.

I started sleeping with a small spiral notebook next to my bed and a tiny flashlight so that I didn't wake up my wife as I woke up to write them down. I then graduated to a digital recorder. My wife didn't seem to mind the noise a few times before I fellasleep.

I also started using a tape recorder in the car, and kept a small spiral notebook in my front shirt pocket for those random meetings with people who have great suggestions.I was able to record many of these great thoughts and ideas. The problem arose when I let those ideas sit and collect dust. When was I supposed to look at them? The notebooks started piling up, and then got filed into a filing cabinet for evaluation sometime in the future.

Once I started having a meeting with myself every week, I realized that this would be the timeto consider and categorize all of the ideas from the past week. I'll go into how to integrate those into your meeting agenda later in the book.

Before I leave this topic of preparation, I want to share a life-changing idea I received from a vendor I worked with many years ago. He carried around a small notebook in his front pocket, and every time he had a thought, or someone gave him an idea,he would write it down. However, the part that was life-changing for me was when he showed me that any time he made a promise to someone, or otherwise created himself a task that needed to be accomplished, he would draw a small empty checkbox next to the item. This way when he went through his notes later, he was able to quickly discern between notes and items of importance that needed to be accomplished.

I have used this technique for many years, and it works great when you're sitting in a meeting or conference taking notes, and something comes to mind that you need to take care of. A small square box is very easy to spot when scanning through your notes in preparation for your weekly meeting. If you use an electronic task software system, asI have for many years, then when you transfer the task from the notebook to the computer you can check it off as being transferred. I hope this idea helps you as much as it has helped me. It's such a small, insignificant idea that radically changed my method of keeping track of important ideas and tasks.

Measure Progress

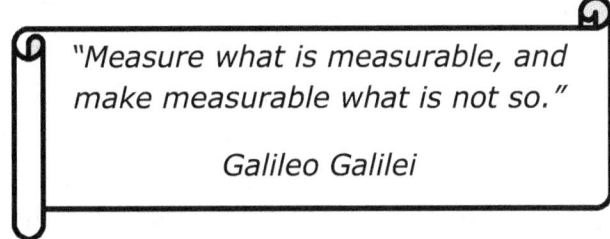

"Measure what is measurable, and make measurable what is not so."

Galileo Galilei

"I'll get that done soon." "Let's get this finished pronto." "I promise to take you to the park another day." "I'll get back with you on that in just a little bit." All of these share the same aspect;they can't be measured. "Soon,""pronto,""another day," and "just a little bit" are all phrasesthat we tend to use when we're either not sure or unwilling to schedule an estimated time of completion.

Walt Disney was well-known for his statement "keep moving forward," which was quoted in the movie "Meet the Robinsons." The full quote that this came from was, "We keep moving forward, opening new doors, and doing new things, because we're curious, and curiosity keeps leading us down new paths." I'm sure we can all agree that moving forward is something that we try to do on a regular basis. Knowing which way is forward happens when we set our goals and head toward them. Knowing whether we are moving in that direction on a week to week basis is accomplished by taking measurements of the steps we are making.

If the goal involves numbers, like selling 100 products before moving on to stage II of some project, then it is fairly easy to quantify and measure the distance in which we're moving forward. It becomes more difficult to measure when the goal is something like, 'improve employee morale,' or, 'get more involved in my teenager's life.' In cases like these we need to break down the goal into smaller tasks that can be measured just by their completion. An example for improving employee morale might be a set of tasks: like, schedule an employee family picnic in two months, spend at least 15 to 20 minutes of quality one-on-one time with each direct report employee. As each of these tasks are completed, you can measure the movement toward your goal and visualize your movement forward.

Study and Compare

> "The early bird gets the worm, but the second mouse gets the cheese."
>
> *Willie Nelson*

You may not have expected to be reading a quote from Willie Nelson in a business book. Well, don't feel alone; I never expected to use a quote from Willie Nelson in a business book. This one was just too funny and too true not to use.

We need to keep a watchful eye on our industry and our competition. In our personal life, we need to keep an eye on what things are competing with our time with our children, spouse, and other family and friends.

In our business life it's imperative that we make wise decisions with regards to our competitors. As CEOs we need to make decisions like whether to become an early adapterof a new technology or not.

I remember when Chase Bank® first came out with the capability of taking a picture of a check with your smart phone to make a deposit into your account. I was talking to my Wells Fargo® bank branch manager, asking when we would be able to do the same thing. She told me that she had been to a meeting recently where the managers were told that the technology had been developed a few years prior, but that they were waiting for another bank to implement it first. Wells Fargo® did not want to be the one to deal with all of the mistakes and potential fraud that can be associated withbecoming the early adapter.

Another example is when Bank of America® became one of the early adaptersin charging a monthly fee for the use of their ATM cards. They had a significant number of customers close their accounts and move to another bank. Many other banks held back to see what would happen when Bank of America® became the first to implement the fee. They became, as the quote states, the second mouse who got the cheese when some of those customers opened up accounts at their bank.

As you go throughout your normal routine every day reading articles, watching television, sitting in meetings, and even just driving down the road, pay attention to any clues that will help you gain a competitive edge with your company, and in the relationships you have with your family members. And then, for goodness sakes, don't forget to write them down so you can bring them to your strategy session!

Your weekly meeting will be the time that you can compare those observations and decide if action needs to be taken. And if action does need to be taken, you can determine what needs to be done, and schedule it.

Press Box View

> *"The trick to forgetting the big picture is to look at everything close-up."*
>
> *Chuck Palahniuk*

Michael Gerber[2], in his book *E-Myth*, discussed the struggle that takes place with the owner of a small business between the three business-related personalities he calls the entrepreneur, the manager, and the technician. The technician wants to focus on the daily activities of business, while the manager maintains order and organization within the company's team.Theentrepreneur sees the business as it could be in

[2]Gerber, M. E. (1995). The E-myth revisited: Why most small businesses don't work and what to do about it. New York: CollinsBusiness

the future. Michael Gerber calls the vantage point of the entrepreneur working *on* your business, not *in* it.

Basically, you need to step away from the daily routine of your business and your personal life in order to gain a more complete perspective. It is true that the forest is very difficult to see when you're right in the middle of it, and all the trees are in the way. It is also difficult to make good business decisions without occasionally stepping away from the politics that often exist in business meetings and the business of daily activities in a family.

My good friend and business mentor, Gary Lockwood, taught me that I needed to run my business from the "press box." He pointed out that during a football game the coach of the team was like a manager in my business. He isthere amongst the players and makesthe calls that need to be made--like when to switch people in and out of positions, and when to pull a player aside to give them a pep talk. Then Gary would explain that the owner of the team was high up in the stadium in his own press box. This was because he could see the "big picture" from up there, and could talk to the head coach with the radio when he spotted something that the coach needed to be aware of.

Your Saturday morning meeting will be youropportunity to sit up in the press box of your life. From there you will be able to view the goals you've set, the mission statement and mantra you have decided to live your life by both personally and professionally, and you will be able to evaluate how quickly you are moving forward.

Chapter 1 Notes…

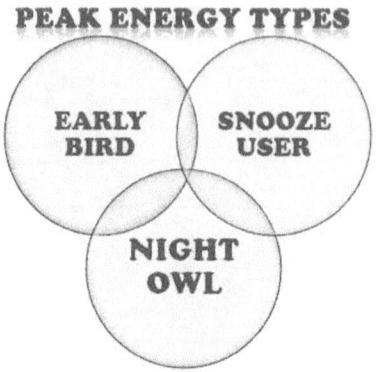

PEAK ENERGY TYPES

EARLY
BIRD

SNOOZE
USER

NIGHT
OWL

CHAPTER TWO

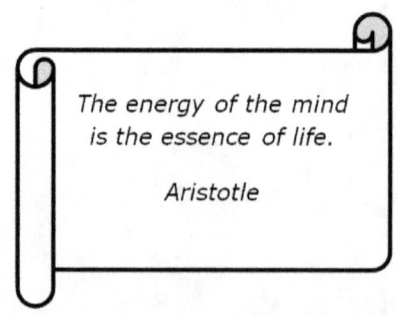

*The energy of the mind
is the essence of life.*

Aristotle

2Peak Energy Type

If you rolled your eyes at the thought of getting up early on Saturday morning to have a meeting with yourself, don't worry--you're not alone. Everyone has different sleep cycles. It is called our circadian rhythm. You may do better having your Saturday morning planning time every Friday night at 10 PM, or Wednesdays at 4pm.

A study done at the University of Alberta[3] using MRI (Magnetic Resonance Imaging)-guided brain stimulation, following participants completing a standardized questionnaire about their habits,was able to determine that 'morning people's' brains were most excitable at nine o'clock in the morning,and'night owl' brains were most excitable at nine o'clock at night. They also discovered that the excitability of reflex pathways that travel through the spinal cord increased throughout the waking period for both groups.

Another study,conducted by researchers at the Université de Liège[4] in Belgium, also using MRI technology, showed that in the lab 'night owls'had a propensity toward longer stamina than early risers. However, the researchers were also quick to explain that early risers, outside of the lab environment, may still

---

[3]Morning people and night owls show significantly different brain function (June 23, 2009). Science Codex

[4] Strickland, E. (April 24, 2009). Night Owls Have More Staying Power Than Early Birds, Brain Study Shows | Discover Magazine

have the advantage over night owls because their circadian rhythms are more aligned with the average working schedule of most businesses in the world.

Ying-Hui Fu[5], a neuroscientist at the University of California, San Francisco and several of her colleagues in San Francisco, Vermont, and Utah, have discovered a mutated gene that seems to be hereditary, which causes drastic circadian rhythm problems. One 49-year-old participant wakes up every morning between 1:30 AM and 4:00 AM with enough energy, in her words, to paint the house. But then about 5:00 PM she is ready for bed and can barely stay awake.

While there are rare cases of extreme circadian rhythm malfunctions, the majority of us can be classified into three distinct peak energy groups. At Saturday Morning CEO, we have called them: early birds, snooze users, and night owls.

Early birds are people who regularly wake up either without an alarm clock or before their alarm clock goes off. Snooze users (which in some cases are night owls in disguise) usually require an alarm clock, a radio, television, and perhaps a nudge from their spouse before they can even see the fog of the morning in front of their eyes. They typically need a shower and breakfast before they can recall the 2+2 equals four. The night owl (I fall into this category) has their greatest burst of energy when most people are getting ready for bed.

---

[5] Roach, J. (March 30, 2005) Early Risers Have Mutated Gene, Study Says| National Geographic News

If you already know when you're peak energy is most prevalent, then you should be able to pick the best time for you to have your "Saturday morning" meeting with yourself. If you are not sure what peak energy type you are, you can either spend some time in a sleep study lab or you can visit: www.SaturdayMorningCEO.com/PET, answer a short questionnaire based on our thorough, yet unscientific research. Your peak energy type will be identified, and you will be given some tips and tricks to help you take full advantage of the time you should set aside.

Chapter 2 Notes…

CHAPTER THREE

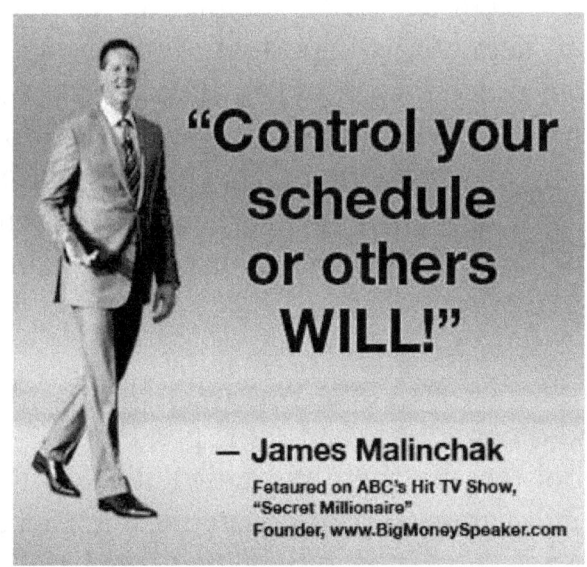

"Control your schedule or others WILL!"

— James Malinchak

Fetaured on ABC's Hit TV Show,
"Secret Millionaire"
Founder, www.BigMoneySpeaker.com

3 Structure of Your 2 Hours

Okay, by now you might be thinking, "This is easy... This guy is just telling me how to get organized and to write down stuff I need to talk about with myself at my meeting each week. It's just way too simple. I really don't need to read the rest the book. All I need to do is set aside a couple hours a week and just sit there and figure stuff out."

When something seems simple we have a human tendency to degrade its importance, and even find ways shortcut the process or avoid it altogether. This is the point in the book where I'm going to ask you to hold on tight and pay close attention. This book is not just some philosophical idea about getting your life focused and moving forward. It is truly an instruction manual for a system that works.

Many people, including you and I at times, have read a book and thought 'that had some great ideas.' Then we put the book on the shelf and either it's still there or it was sold at a garage sale or donated to the friends of the local library. I hope that right now you will feel like you're sitting across from me face-to-face and feeling the desire that I have for you to put these recommendations into action.

This chapter addresses the overall structure and framework for your strategic planning meeting. Subsequent chapters cover the agenda items themselves.

Focus

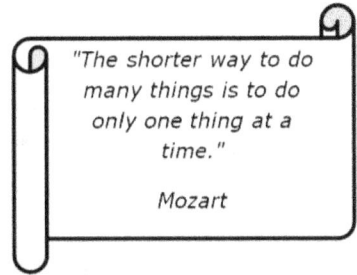

"The shorter way to do many things is to do only one thing at a time."

Mozart

Have you ever tried to focus on a picture that is not in focus? Take a look at the picture below:

If you look closely enough you can see from the circles and the droplets of light that these are small candles. Because the picture is out of focus, it might be a very difficult task to count how many candles are in the picture. Trying hard to focus, you might notice that it looks like at least one or two of the candles near the back left of the picture are not even lit. Even if you are in front of these candles in person, you would have difficulty focusing on all of them at the same time. You have to pick out just one candle at a time and look at it with greater attention. The candle on the bottom right of this picture is somewhat in focus through the camera's lens.

This photograph should be an example to all of us on how we should accomplish a large number of tasks and complete the goals and dreams that we have in our personal and business lives. We can only take on one thing at a time.

My father, who passed away in August of 2005, had a saying that if somebody asks you what time it is, you should not tell them how to build a watch. When we communicate a point to someone it needs to be simple and understandable. This includes when we communicate with ourselves.

It's not unrealistic to think that there must be,at minimum, tens of thousands of thoughts that pass through our mind every week. Trying to get a grasp or understanding of all of them at the same time is impossible. Just like in the picture of the candles, we can only truly focus on one item at a time. But, we can't take the risk of losing sight of all the rest of the thoughts while looking at just the one. This is exactly why there's such a tremendous need for a weekly strategic planning meeting with yourself. Ideas must be captured and recorded, and then brought up in an orderly fashion.

The most important detail about your weekly strategy meetings is the detail most business leaders try to take shortcuts around. That detail is the written agenda, which is the real foundation for your weekly meeting.

I have read hundreds of self-improvement and business books over the years, and you have probably done the same. A large majority of those books motivated me, and discussed the answers to a lot of *why* questions. *Why* I should want to get more organized, *why* I should involve my employees in more company-related decisions, *why* I should consider franchising, *why* it's good to buy when the market is down. But, not many of those books answered the **how** questions. The majority of this book is dedicated to answering the how question of holding your weekly strategic planning meeting with yourself. In fact, every item on the agenda will be discussed in the next few chapters.

Agenda

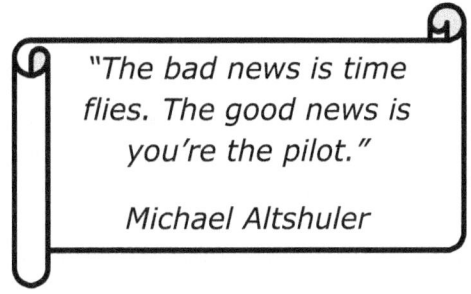

"*The bad news is time flies. The good news is you're the pilot.*"

Michael Altshuler

Come with me for just a moment, to a time when you had to put something together with a set of instructions. Taking the liberty of general stereotyping, men have a tendency to set aside the instructions and try to put it together using what we like to call 'common sense.' The majority the time, as we all know, extra screws are left over, or for some reason the new bookshelf just won't sit level, or one piece is on backwards. It may *work* without the instructions, but it will take twice as long; and at least part of it may need to be reassembled more than once until it fits perfectly.

Your written agenda is that set of instructions for your strategic planning meeting. It will serve as a checklist, a tool to measure your progress, and a written record for later review and evaluation. It would be impossible to accomplish a single one of these without a formal written agenda.

Here is a very simplified outline to use as a framework for your meeting agenda. The times listed on this agenda will not be accurate for your first few meetings, but are a good guideline touse once you establish a routine and have a system figured out that works best for you.

Opening (5 minutes)

1. Life Balance (15 minutes)

2 Mission/Vision Review (5 minutes)

3 Goals (15 minutes)

4 Personal SWOT (15 minutes)

5 Innovations (15 minutes)

6 Action Plan (20 minutes)

7 Evaluation (15 minutes)

Closing & "Hammock Time" (15 minutes)

(Download a sample agenda at
SaturdayMorningCEO.com/forms)

> *"One worthwhile task carried to a successful conclusion is worth half-a-hundred half-finished tasks."*
>
> *Malcolm S. Forbes*

The World Health Organization (WHO) took notice of the worldwide problem with morbidity rate in surgery. They undertook several studies to determine what would be the best way to increase surgical success rates. A large number of studies were done considering a variety of factors. The findings were surprising to some. The WHO discovered that the very best way to decrease surgical errors and reduce morbidity rate was to implement a checklist. In 2009, WHO produced and distributed their implementation manual of the surgical safety checklist[6].

Come to find out, the same idea used by airline pilots for many years to ensure safety of a flight prior to take off with a preflight checklist was the best idea for surgery as well.

Is your business or personal life so much less important than keeping an airplane in the air or providing for a safe surgical environment that you think a written

---

[6]http://whqlibdoc.who.int/publications/2009/9789241598590_eng.pdf

agenda is not necessary? It normally takes 8 to 12 weeks of using your written agenda at your weekly meeting to overcome the temptationtouse a scribbled-on piece of paper in place of a formal written agenda.

Evaluations of the implementation of the WHO surgical checklist have been conducted in Finland[7] and the Netherlands[8]. These two studies, along with many others done around the world, discovered that the resulting improvements using the checklist varied depending on compliance to the checklist by the surgical staff. Several of the implementation studies found that staff felt they had atleast parts of the checklist memorized after using it a few times. This resulted in some of the items on the checklist being overlooked, when they started checking off boxes without reading them.

Changing to a new way of doing things is almost always awkward. I'd like to demonstrate this by asking you to take a quick break from reading and cross your arms in front of you. Now, look down and see which arm is on top of the other. Is it your left arm or your right arm? Next, re-fold your arms so that the opposite arm is on top. Does that feel comfortable? I didn't think so. We're all such creatures of habit that change is

---

[7]Takala, R., Pauniaho, S., Kotkansalo, A., Helmiö, P., Blomgren, K., Helminen, M., & ... Ikonen, T. (2011). A pilot study of the implementation of WHO surgical checklist in Finland: improvements in activities and communication. Acta Anaesthesiologica Scandinavica, 55(10), 1206-1214.

[8]van Klei, W., Hoff, R., van Aarnhem, E., Simmermacher, R., Regli, L., Kappen, T., & ... Peelen, L. (2012). Effects of the introduction of the WHO "Surgical Safety Checklist" on in-hospital mortality: a cohort study. Annals Of Surgery, 255(1), 44-49.

something we have to *want* to do. Using a formal written agenda for a meeting that you have all by yourself may seem way out in left field from the normal way of doing things. But, I promise, once you make this change and it becomes a habit, you will realize the benefits as you start successfully accomplishing the goals and tasks on your checklist.

Measurable

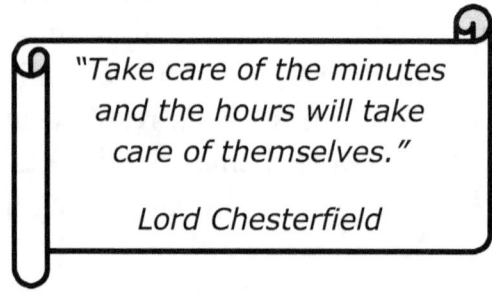

"Take care of the minutes and the hours will take care of themselves."

Lord Chesterfield

We would never consider going to the hardware store to buy new window blinds without first having measured the windows. In addition, it would be impossible to imagine an NFL football game where both teams decided they would just play until they got tired, not keep score and give the umpire the night off. No, they want to measure their success every inch of the way as they compete with the other team.

I now have grown children and remember the doorway that we used to have,where our children stood up and got measured to see how tall they were. Little horizontal marks were drawn with their initials next to it. I'm guessing that you're familiar with this process. You either have children of your own who you are measuring,or you have some marks with your initials next to them on your parent's doorway from years ago. Our doorway has long been painted over and we have moved from that house to our small five-acre ranch. However, the whole idea of comparing and measuring has not gone away. My son Daniel has grown just a little bit taller than me. We still take every possible opportunity to stand back to back and verify who is taller. This is officially the first time I have publicly admitted that he is taller than I am. It has been fun measuring our children in their anatomical stature. However, it has been much more fulfilling to measure how they are growing into dedicated and honest adults.

Scientists and other members of academia continually find new ways to measure as many parts of the human experience as feasibly possible. There was even a scale developed for the Mature Adult Profile[9] (MAP) bySusann Cook-Greuter that was used as a basis in a case study[10] measuring the transformation of a leader in an organization.

If you want to be able to evaluate and measure your own personal progression towards your goals,you need to be able to measure your forward mobility. Setting aside two hours a week and doing a little planning for it, and maintaining a written agenda, keeping track of thedecisions made during the meeting, will help you

[9]http://www.springerlink.com/content/v4l3p3562l681u06/

[10]Metcalf, M., & Lipetz, R. (2009). Transforming a Leader and his Organization: An Approach, a Case Study, and Measurable Results. Integral Leadership Review, 1-16

measure your success.

While I'm a strong proponent on the idea of having a formal written agenda, I will be realistic and saying that keeping formal minutes from your meetings is not necessary. You will have action items that quickly become prioritized tasks and calendar items. The key to making this successful is developing a system that works best for you in transitioning the decisions from your meeting into tasks, and then accomplishments in the week ahead.

Mentor Trackable

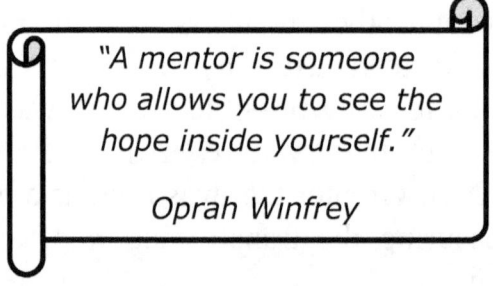

"A mentor is someone who allows you to see the hope inside yourself."

Oprah Winfrey

You have probably discovered, as I have, that having a business coach or mentor can often be the critical ingredient for success. This is also true in your personal life. You might even have more than one to enhance a particular area of your personal or business life. I'll talk to one mentor if I'm in need of some legal advice, another for investment advice, and still others for marketing, sales, emotional, spiritual, and fitness advice.

The agendas from your meeting, along with the notes that you take, are great tools you can share with your mentor(s). During my monthly meetings with

GaryLockwood, my business mentor, there were occasions when he left my office after a great session, and not 15 minutes later I would remember something that I really wanted to ask him. Keeping track of your agendais a great way to remember what you wanted to bring up with your mentor. I would even suggest going as far as using a specific colored highlighter to mark mentor-discussion items.

The interactions with your mentor can also work in the other direction. The meeting you have with your mentor is typically a golden opportunity for new ideas, strategies, and considerations. They should all be recorded and carried over to your next week's strategic planning meeting.

Open/Close Routine

> "Opening & closing ceremonies at the Olympics set apart the events as significant and important. Make your planning time a significant event by doing the same."
>
> W. Denis Nurmela

An important ingredient of creating a productive weekly meeting is to develop some traditions that will make the meeting become familiar and comfortable. The sooner you can make your meeting a habit, the better for your productivity.

As a speaker and corporate trainer I have learned that the most memorable parts of my talk to the audience are the opening and closing remarks. While there are some tricks to creating highlights in the body of the talk, you can destroy a talk by having a weak opening or closing. One of the very early steps in setting up our Saturday Morning radio show was the station manager helping us pick out the theme song to play at the beginning of every show. Just like a television show or movie has an opening theme song, anything in life that we want to become familiar is more easily remembered when it starts out the same way every time.

In an effort to help create the habit of this meeting every week as quickly as possible, it is important that you create a memorable opening and closing for your meeting. The opening and closing of your meeting should stir your life's passion.

While I have not spent much time on this topic in this book, it is imperative that we have some passion for our business and personal life's growth and success. Each of us are very different, and our passions are kindled in different ways.

You might have a song that motivates you. You should listen to it at the beginning of each meeting, or you may choose to take a minute or two looking at your favorite family photo at the end of every meeting to help inspire you and your personal goals. Some of us are spiritually motivated, and would do well with an opening and closing prayer at the meetings. You may want to create a shortlist of your favorite inspirational quotes to read before or after your meeting. The possibilities are limitless. It's really based on your personal method of stimulating your passion for your business and personal goals.

The key is that you do the same thing every meeting! I am old enough to remember standing up in elementary school and reciting the Pledge of Allegiance to the United States of America every morning before a day of classes. This was followed by announcements from the principal and other matters that needed to be dealt with for the day. This routine helped create a pattern for learning. Standing with our right hand over our heart and looking at the flag as we recited the Pledge of Allegiance prepared my brain for the events that would follow because every school day began exactly the same.

Spend some time considering what type of opening and closing will work best for you at your strategic planning meetings. You really want to chose something that will help keep you focused on your goals and passions in life. This meeting will become more and more important to you as time goes on. Coming up with a good opening and closing activity will give the meeting a feeling of ceremonial importance.

Daily Journaling with Purpose

"Journal writing is a voyage to the interior."

Christina Baldwin

Keeping a journal comes in many different formats. Some of us journal all of our daily activities in the format of a handwritten or electronic diary. Others use checklists, voice recorders, or even the infamous Post-it notes.

If you do not already use one of these methods and are still relying on that biological database between your ears, then let me suggest that you consider choosing something a little more reliable.

Whatever method you use to record your thoughts, ideas, and suggestions from others, you should now start doing so with a new purpose. Recording possible agenda items for your next week's strategic business meeting should be one of your top priorities in journaling during the week.

The day before your strategic planning meeting you will look through your recorded thoughts and decide what needs to be on the upcoming agenda. You may even want to scan through the list more frequently than just once a week. Because, invariably, additional supporting ideas will come to you as you review the list. If you have reviewed the list a few days before your meeting,then the idea itself may do some transforming just because you looked at it more than once.

Habit Forming / Trusted System

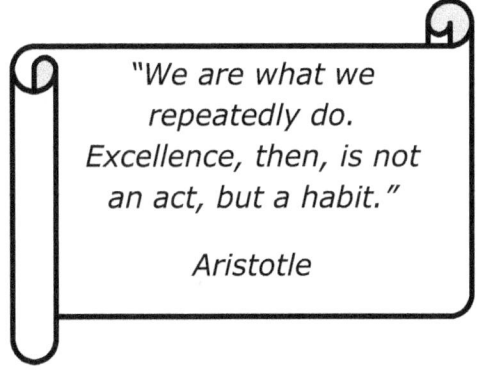

"We are what we repeatedly do. Excellence, then, is not an act, but a habit."

Aristotle

When was the last time that you had to stop and think about how to tie your shoes?Do you have to stop and think about which button to press on your alarm clock every morning? Our brain is wired in such a way that it remembers things that we repeat over and over. This process of remembering or creating a habit helps us to utilize our brain energy on more creative aspects of our life, and allows mundane and routine activities to be handled by our unconscious mind.

The first several times that you have this strategic planning meeting with yourself, you may want to follow along with this book. I promise you, it will feel different as you begin the process of making this meeting a regular part of your life. Repeating the process over and over again will allow you to have the logistics of the meeting become like tying your shoes, something you don't have to think about a lot. Then you'll be able to spend more time on the creative and decisivepowers you should be using during the meeting. The actual structure of the meeting will start taking care of itself.

Chapter 3 Notes…

CHAPTER FOUR

"The key to keeping your balance is knowing when you've lost it."

Anonymous

4 Agenda Item: Life Balance

As a CEO, I have attended many conferences, read many books, and listened to many audio presentations that tout the importance of creating life balance. I agree with this 100%. However, the majority of the information was explaining *why* we need life balance rather than *how* to obtain balance in our lives.

Your Saturday morning meeting is not just a meeting for business, nor is it just a meeting for your personal, or family life. It is a meeting inclusive of all of the above. This is the earliest planning stage for all other meetings and encounters that you will be having with others whichwill take place during the course of the upcoming week.

In his book *Seedsof Greatness*, Denis Waitley[11] introduced an exercise called the wheel of fortune. He asks a series of questions that the reader answers, and then placesthe resulting score on a circular chart. The scores are then connected to one another with lines. The goal was to create as round a wheel as possible, with balanced ratio scores between the various categories, representing different aspects of your life.

Completing the assessment of the wheel of fortune is something I would suggest that you do, or at least complete something similar. This will help you identify areas that you may need to increase attention to during

---

[11]Waitley, D. (1983). Seeds of greatness: the ten best-kept secrets of total success. Old Tappan, N.J.: Revell.

your Saturday morning meetings.

Prioritize

> "If you want to make good use of your time, you've got to know what's most important and then give it all you've got."
>
> Lee Iacocca

In the corporate world we learn how to create a **SWOT** analysis to identify the **S**trengths, **W**eaknesses, **O**pportunities, and **T**hreats related to our businesses. You're going to learn how to do a SWOT analysis on all aspects of your life in a later chapter. Right here I want to talk about making sure that you put what's important on your agenda.

Earlyin my marriage, it quickly came to my attention that I placed a much higher priority on appointments I had with clients, vendors, and other business associates than with my wife. Following the examples of others, I decided that it was time for me to raise the priority on my relationship with my wife. This was accomplished by creating a weekly date night. When our children were much younger and finances were tight, a date night sometimes consisted of a trip to a local fast food restaurant to split a pack of french fries. I remember that many of the dates we went on early in our marriage cost us more in babysitting fees than in the activity we decided to do for the date. What we did on the date was never as important as the fact that we were having a date in the first place.

Then, somethingbeyond miraculous started to happen with our relationship. While our date nights did not create endless bliss with never a problem to arise again, it did help me see the importance of actually scheduling time to be with my wife, just like I did with business contacts. When we first started having the date nights, I believe it was Tuesday nights that were the discount night at the movie theater. Tuesday nights were a great opportunity for us to spend some quality time together.

But the miraculous part of having a date night every week was that our communication with one another the rest of the week also improved. We both seemed to know instinctively that we were going to have some time within the next 4 to 5 days to spend with one another on a date. Some of the frustrations we might have vented to one another during the rest of the week were put off until Tuesday. When Tuesday night came around it was much easier to discuss the issue after some time had passed, and quite often whatever the source of frustration may have been seemed to disappear over the days we waited for date night.

I could probably count on one hand only how many times we missed a weekly date night since we started them around 1996. In fact, when I have had to be out of town for business for a week or more at a time we might find two nights the following week to go do something together. I share this story with you because it was a result of identifying a priority that I needed to change.

Rather than just telling myself over and over again that I needed to find a way to focus more on that priority, I turned it into a task that could be followed through with, measured, and recorded. Okay, I'll be very honest--we did not record it anywhere, but we were definitely aware--and still are--of whether we have been out each week on a date night or not.

Speaking of measuring a task that relates to something personal, someone gave us an idea,when our children were young,that we called 'special time.' Each month, each of our six children would receive one-on-one time with mom and with dad individually. At first we started with a simple chart on the refrigerator. It could easily be checked off after we completed a one-on-one event with a child.

It never had to be anything big, like a trip to an amusement park. It was usually a trip to the gas station to fill up the car, and may have involved the purchase of some candy while we were there. Our children got creative as they grew older, and at least one of them started putting checkmarks on other people's boxes for the month. This way they would be "next up" for special time that month. We had to reexamine the system and make some modifications. The chart remained, but the boxes got bigger so we could write down what we did together in the box. This was much more difficult to counterfeit.

At the writing of this book, our children are either teenagers or adults with families of their own. Special time is not high on their priority list any longer, and it has become a good memory. But hopefully they will implement some similar practices with their own children as time goes on.

My point is that priorities change, as do the motivators for those who are involved in relationships and activities that need to be prioritized. Your personal, family, social, faith, and community life, as well as all aspects within your business life, should be in writing on your agenda to identify them as prioritiesso you can create doable tasks related to them.

Quick Rating

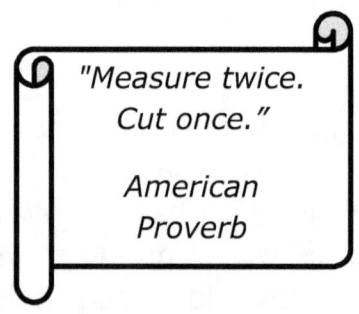

"Measure twice.
Cut once."

American
Proverb

Larger companies take the SWOT analysis and give a value to each of the identified items. This is accomplished through what is called the External Factor Analysis Summary (EFAS), and the Internal Factor Analysis Summary (IFAS). If you are an experienced CEO, then you're familiar with theprocess of providing a weight and rating to each item listed in the categories of **Strengths**, **Weaknesses**, **Opportunities**, and **Threats**. These weights and ratings are then calculated into a weighted score. Those scores are then compared with one another, and items with the highest score will receive the most attention.

While a SWOT analysis should be a part of your Saturday morning meeting agenda, the internal and external factor summary analyses can be a little overboard for this weekly meeting. However, I have worked as a business consultant to some very analytical thinkers. So if you feel that you want to take the analysis a step further, by all means please do so. It really depends on you as an individual, and the degree of diversified responsibilities you have.

I have found that a simple and quick scoring system is all that is usually necessary for this Saturday morning strategic planning meeting. Some people prefer prioritizing topics and tasks with ABC ratings: A - being the highest rating or most pressing and C - being something that might be able to wait until at least next week's meeting. Others feel more comfortable with a rating scale of 1 to 10.

Either rating system will work perfectly for your Saturday morning strategy session. All you need to do is place the rating down the left-hand side of the agenda before you start your meeting, maybe even the day before. This will help you balance the time you spent on each item based on the rating that you gave it.

Often times during this meeting, in fact quite often, you will become compelled to spend extra time on a few of the items. If they are rated with an A then go ahead and spend the time on them. If they are rated with a B or a C you may want to jot a couple notes down next to them and move them forward to next week's agenda. Next week it might become an A priority, and then you can spend more time on it.

Focus on Strengths

> "A man should never be appointed into a managerial position if his vision focuses on people's weaknesses rather than on their strengths." Peter Drucker

I remember being taught as a young child that I could do anything I put my mind to. If I did not have skills in a specific area, I could work hard and learn what I needed to become strong in thatarea. I have found that this is commonly taught to children, and even shared with adults. While there is some truth to this, it's also very important for us to understand that we can't do everything, and that each of us isunique and have a propensity toward specific skills.

In high school I was a runner. I was determined to do well as a sprinter. I consistently practiced improving my speeds on the 50 yard dash, and also enjoyed participating in short relays. I could not understand why my coach kept recommending that I try running with the cross-country team. The idea of running further than 100 yards at that time was not very exciting to me in my early high school years. As kind as my coach was in making the recommendation, I now realize as an adult that behind his encouraging words was the knowledge that I was just not cut out to be a sprinter. It was not one of my strengths.

Finally, being convinced that cross-country would somehow help me become a better sprinter, I decided to run with the cross-country team. All it took was once and I was hooked. Through my mid-20s I would regularly run 6 miles every morning, and had no problem running a 10 km race in about 45 min. I was so glad to have been encouraged by my coach to follow my strengths rather than try to overcome a weakness.

When you clearly know what your strengths are, it ismuch easier to decide which tasks are better delegated to someone who has a strength in your area of weakness,and which tasks you should take on yourself. The old idea of,"if it's going to be done right I have to do it myself" is just going to create stress and imbalance in your life.

Henry Ford was once asked to what he attributed his success. He explained that he continually evaluated the areas in whichhe was weak and hired people who had strengths in those areas,making sure to listen to their advice. It's very important for you to spend the time discovering where your strengths are, and to know where your weaknesses are. Some companies regularly use the Myers-Briggs personality tests as a measurement device. This is helpful in determining how to communicate with people that you work with or interact with in your personal life, but in my opinion is not the very best way to specifically find out what your strengths are.

Although I do recommend finding out as much about yourself as you can--and the Myers-Briggs is one of many ways to help identify what kind of person you are.

For the purpose of this weekly meeting I would highly suggest that you obtain a copy of *Strengths Finder 2.0*[12]. The book itself is a companion to an online questionnaire that will help identify your strengths. After completing the survey, spend some time reading the description of each strength in the book. I would recommend that you keep those strengths written down on your agenda so you can look at them every week. If you have also completed a Myers-Briggs or other self-assessment then you should list those results on your agenda as well. By listing them on the agenda it makes it quick and easy to find them and to keep them in consideration as you develop measurable goals and create tasks during your Saturday morning meeting.

---

[12]Rath, T. (2007). Strengths finder 2.0. New York: Gallup Press

Chapter 4 Notes…

CHAPTER FIVE

"I can teach anybody how to get what they want out of life. The problem is that I can't find anybody who can tell me what they want."

Mark Twain

5 Agenda Item: Mission/Vision

If your company has living, breathing mission and vision statements,whichare constantly referred to when making decisions in board meetings, consider yourself one of the lucky few. You have probably seen, like I have, mission and vision statements that can only be found in the policy and procedure manual, or in rare occasions in a frame on the wall. Usually that frame is covered in dust, and if you asked the majority of people who work for the company *what* their mission statement is, or even *where* it is, they may not be able to tell you.

The intent of this book is not to spend a lot of time explaining how to write mission and vision statements, or what exactly they should entail. However, know that having solid mission and vision statements which reflect the goals of the company as a whole is very important. These two statements should be either on your agenda every week or at least be with you during the meeting so you can review them.

Okay, we talked about business mission/vision statements. Now it's time to talk about a statement for yourself and your family.

It will help you tremendously to sit down both by yourself and with anyone else who is a valuable part of your life and discuss the goals that you have for the future. The next step toward determining your overall life vision statement is to identify what inner core values are necessary for you to obtain the goals you came up with.

A common question asked by business clients is: What's the difference between a mission statement and a vision statement? The vision statement for either your personal life or your company is where you see yourself and your business in the future in relationship to your values, core competencies, and goals. The mission statement is a description of your life and your business in the present tense,and describes how you operate on a day-to-day basis to reach, and become, the description laid out in your vision statement.

As you refer to your personal and business mission and vision statements each week, you will find yourself having a greater focus and understanding of where your energies should be utilized. Many of my clients, after going through theprocess of creating mission and vision statements for themselves and their business, found that some of the activities they had been involved in were outside of the parameters they set in these statements.

Opportunities to introduce new products or services in a business or to implement new activities in family and social relationships come quite often. We can easily get distracted chasing the shiny things in life and get completely off course from our goals, and sometimes even our inner core values. I really enjoyed the 2009 Disney® movie *Up*. I don't think I'll ever forget how quickly the dogs in the movie got distracted when they saw a squirrel. I'm even laughing right now as I'm writing this paragraph. Trying to keep up a garden and a small orchard of fruit trees on our 5+ acres, I myself become quickly distracted when I see a squirrel, a gopher, or a rabbit trying to compete with my family for food. I become easily distracted,and even forget what my original purpose was out on the property.

Unless your squirrel/distraction is a very high priority emergency that needs to be dealt with immediately, your first point of action should be to identify the distraction and see whether it even conforms to your mission statement and vision statement. Otherwise, resist every temptation to chase the squirrel, because it will take you away from your life's goals.Perhapsonly by a degree or two, but over a distance of time even one degree takes you in a direction not completely aligned with your goals, mission statement, and vision statement.

Source of Passion

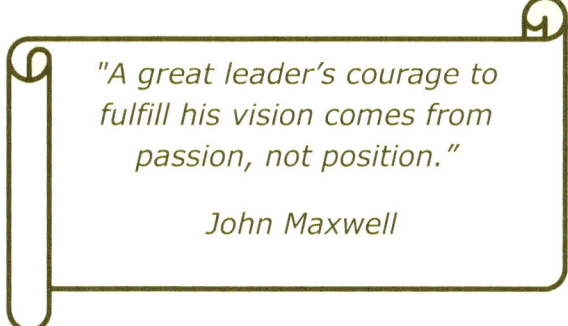

"A great leader's courage to fulfill his vision comes from passion, not position."

John Maxwell

When mission and vision statements are aligned with inner core values, there is a pretty good chance that any efforts made moving towards them will invoke a sense of passion deep inside of you. I think it's really important for me to hit on a point right now that could become a point of conflict if we don't discuss it.

Depending on whether you are the founding CEO of your company or the sitting CEO, you may or may not have been involved in your company's mission and vision statements. I do understand that you may be working for a company that does not have goals in 100% alignment with your personal and family goals. But, I'm not talking about completely misaligned values. If, for instance, you are a strong advocate for non-smoking laws, and happen to have a job as CEO of a tobacco company, then you need to make a values-based decision and get out of there... Yesterday!

The dilemma that I'm talking about is much more subtle, and can be described as feeling motivated towards company goals and visions, but not feeling great energies of passion toward them. If you feel that this is your situation, identify whether or not your business goals will at least provide you with the means of obtaining your personal goals. Your personal goals then would be the true source of your passion and energy to drive yourself toward accomplishing even the business goals.

If you're having trouble finding the passion in either your business or personal goals right now, it's time to sit down and reevaluate what your goals should be. All the ideas and procedures I'm sharing with you in this book will only walk you through the steps of creating a more focused, purposeful, and productive life. Identifying your passion and knowing where your passion reservoir is are essential steps in not only becoming more productive,but enjoying life while doing it.

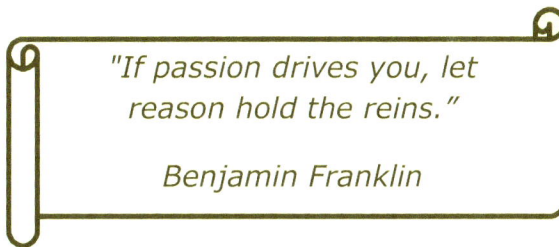

"If passion drives you, let
reason hold the reins."

Benjamin Franklin

You just read how important passion is. If you just sped through the last section without it touching you inside a little bit, then you might want to go back and read again a little slower. Once you understand what drives you to do what you do, it's time to start understanding what to do when you do what you do. (Try saying that three times fast) You, like I, have probably had days when you felt you were practicing "fireman management style." Unexpected deadlines, a major stakeholder with an urgent request, or a potentially damaging public relations situation can take us off track from the very best planning strategy in the world.

The Saturday morning meeting system is not intended to fix every problem, but itcan help to create a greater sense of focus, and helps to set parameters which can be used when deciding if the squirrel can be ignored, just observed, or must be dealt with immediately. Part of the analysis process in the Saturday morning meeting is to identify actions that have been taken the week before and assess how changes can be made when similar situations arise in the future.

You will not completely solve *any* problems that involve interactions with others during your Saturday morning meeting. Remember, you're only meeting with yourself. What the meeting is intended to do is give you the time you need to identify what your role will be in the meeting or conversation that you will have with others who are involved.

As an example in your personal life: Let's say you are having a problem with a teenage son or daughter. During your personal strategic planning meeting you may come up with the idea of a written contract with your child, or some type of incentive program for good behavior. You will have an opportunity during your Saturday morning meeting to clarify your thoughts and feelings regarding the situation, and should even jot down some notes about your ideas. Later, when you get some time to speak with your spouse or your child, you can discover their ideas on the subject and compare them with yours. You will be able to come up with a much better solution than if you tried to deal with the situation in the spur of the moment without any advanced planning.

An example in your business life might be an upcomingcontract negotiation with a new vendor. During your personal strategic meeting you can identify the important points you want to address during the negotiation. You can make much wiser decisions during your Saturday morning time slot (whenever that may be for you) than if you were to take 15 minutes before the negotiation with the vendor to gather your thoughts.

This section is not just about thefocus of your ideas, but also discusses alignment. The ideas you come up with during your personal strategic planning meeting should always be in line with your mission and vision statements, both personal and business. This is accomplished by running the ideas through the filter of your mission and vision statements. Unless it is a very complicated and involved decision, the process of making sure your ideas are in alignment does not take very long at all. It is, however, an essential step to make sure that you are on track and headed forward directly toward your goals, and not off course by 1 or 2 degrees.

Look Through Different Lenses

> "Life is like a landscape. You live in the midst of it, but can describe it only from the vantage point of distance."
>
> Charles Lindbergh

Theoffice where you conduct business can be a very busy place, and very lonely at the same time. The same is true of a busy household. I shared the story previously about my wife and I taking special time with each of our children once a month. It was amazing how different each of our children were when it was just a one-on-one interaction. When they were away from all the competition that existed in the household we actually got to know them better.

Thisis true of ourselves individually as well. We really need to get away for just a couple of hours from the busyness of life to get to know what our inner core values really are, what our goals are, where we would like to see our relationships go, and where we want to take our business in the future.

In addition to using this time at the meeting to get to know our own self better, we can also put on a different set of glasses as we approach some of the items on the agenda. To be more specific, we can imagine ourselves as our customer, as our spouse, or as a child and try to view the issue from their point of view. This is easier to do during this quieter time you have set aside for this meeting.

Chapter 5 Notes…

CHAPTER SIX

"Make at least one definite move daily toward your goal."

Bruce Lee

6 Agenda Item: Goals

At this point in your meeting, when you see goalson the agenda, it will not only be time for you to review them, but also to evaluate if they are still valid. Goals should be subject to change so they reflect the current desires we have for our future business and personal achievements. They also should be changed as we complete them.

I remember in college during one of my degree programs we discussed the plight of Nike® wanting to become the number one shoe manufacturer. They were up against Adidas,® and they actually reach their goal. The problem arose when they did not set a new one. It did not take long for other companies to surpass them in sales.

Any goals that you have listed on your agenda that are not personal, but somehow involve a family member, a business partner, or other individual, should be the goals that were determined in a conversation or meeting you had with them regarding these goals. Working together with others on common goals is essential to their success. The only reason you have them on this agenda is so that you can evaluate your role and responsibilities individually toward achieving them. If in the course of this meeting with yourself you think of something that should be discussed with other stakeholders, then you should create an action item or task to share that information with them.

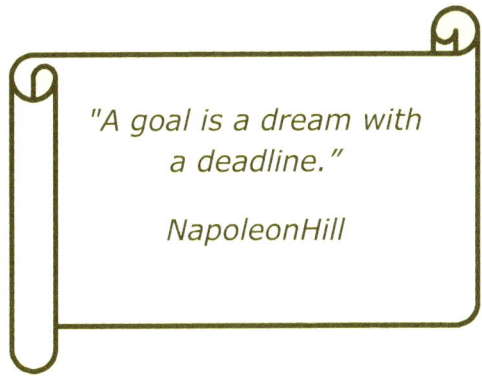

"A goal is a dream with
a deadline."

NapoleonHill

Napoleon Hill has a good point with this quote. However, I would take it one step further and say, "A goal is a dream that is written down and has a deadline."

This portion of your agenda is when you will review your personal and family goals. Personal goals might include anything from overcoming avice, to working to improve a relationship, or some personal financial goal. Family goals, here on this agenda, should just be a carryover from goals that you set with your spouse and/or children. The reason they are on your agenda for this meeting with yourself is that you can assess your own personal role and responsibility toward achieving those goals, and create new tasks as you completeothers.

Business goals are typically tied to a very large number of measurable milestones whichare clearly defined and delegated to different departments in the company, and individuals who take responsibility for their portion of achieving the goal. With personal and family goals, measurable milestones may be more difficult to define. A personal or family goal that is financial in nature is fairly easy to set measurable milestones on. However, if the goal is to build a stronger relationship with a child, as an example, then identifying the activities that should be put into place to help strengthen the relationship is the first step in creating something measurable.

Let's say you decided to be home a little bit sooner in the evenings to join the family for dinner, because you felt this would help to strengthen that relationship. Keeping track of how many times you came home earlier to share dinner with the family would create something that is measurable. Use your imagination and creativity as you create tasks that you feel will bring you closer to your personal and family goals. Just remember to make them something that you can measure, and not to use vague terms like,"I'll be home early for dinner more often than usual." Instead, pick a certain number of days per week that you intend to be home early for dinner. Then track that and evaluate it during your weekly meeting.

Business

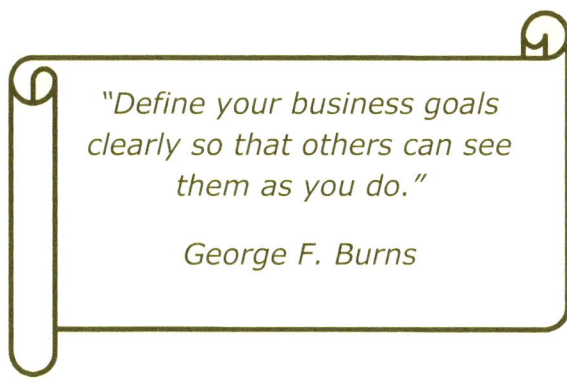

As CEO of the company you have a different set of responsibility towards business goals than you do family goals. Business goals are usually tied to a matrix of detailed and measurable steps necessary to obtain the goals. They are listed on your personal strategic meeting agenda so you can identify any areas where emphasis needs to be redirected, and to make sure that your personal contribution toward these goals is sufficient to see the goals through to a successful conclusion.

As CEO you have the primary responsibility of communicating the mission and vision statements and goals to your management and employees. This item on your agenda should also be a self-assessment process for how well you are communicating these goals toothers. Use this time to look inward rather than just looking at the reports that are coming back from others' activities related to the goals listed.

Chapter 6 Notes…

CHAPTER SEVEN

"Change the changeable, accept the unchangeable, and remove yourself from the unacceptable."

Denis Waitley

7 Agenda Item: Personal SWOT

If you are a seasoned CEO, then a SWOT analysis should be fairly second nature to you in relationship to your business affairs. If you are an entrepreneur who is starting a new business, then this maybe some new terminology for you. But don't feel out of place, because even the seasoned CEO has probably never attempted or even thought about doing a SWOT analysis on personal or family endeavors.

This is probably a good time to recommend another book to you. If you like the idea of thinking about yourself as a business entity and applying business principles to your life, then you should consider reading *Me Inc.*[13] Scott Ventrella applies Fortune 500 company practices to an individual person. It is not a book intended just for CEOs or even managers, but for anyone who may be looking for a job, thinking about changing careers, or venturing out on any set of decisions. Scott suggests that we assess ourselves as we would assess our companies and establish the value that we give to others around us.

A SWOT analysis can be easily explained as the internal and external evaluation and analysis of a company, an individual, or even a relationship. Strengths and weaknesses are internal factors that are considered

---

[13]Ventrella, S. W. (2007). ME, Inc., how to master the business of being you: a personalized program for exceptional living. Hoboken, N.J.: John Wiley & Sons

during this analysis and they are the two areas that we have some control over. Opportunities and threats, on the other hand, are external factors that we consider, and we typically don't have very much, if any, control over these.

Strengths / Weaknesses

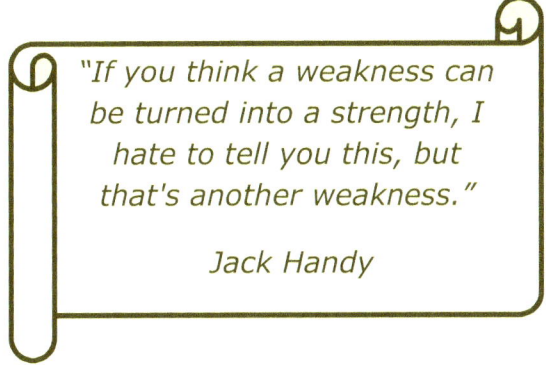

"If you think a weakness can be turned into a strength, I hate to tell you this, but that's another weakness."

Jack Handy

The personal strengths that you will examineat this point on the agenda should have been well defined through the strengths finder assessment tool and book the goes along with it. This is the time in the agenda when you will evaluate the tasks that you created, or even the challenges that you have identified, and measure them against your strengths. If you are the analytical type, then you may want to look up how to use a TOWS (SWOT backwards) Matrix. It is a systematic way of comparing internal and external aspects of the SWOT analysis.

Business strengths should have been determined at a prior corporate strategic planning meeting. You would have them listed here only so you can evaluate your participation in them. Business strengths and weaknesses are best determined with many of the stakeholders involved in the process.

The identification of personal weaknesses should not become an opportunity to think about what steps should be taken to strengthen these weaknesses;instead, you just need to identify them as weaknesses and accept them. It does not mean that they need to remain your weaknesses forever;it just means that you will avoid making a mistake byassigning yourself a task that would require you to be strong in an area that you're not.

Opportunities / Threats

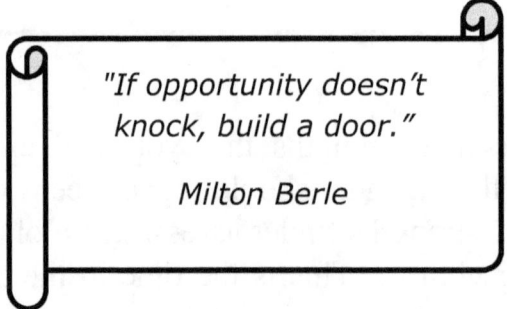

"If opportunity doesn't knock, build a door."

Milton Berle

An ancient American Indian saying is "You can't step into the same river twice." The water keeps changing the river as it flows. This is so very true, and should keep you alert every week when you consider opportunities and threats in both your personal and business life. Milton Berle's quote has been one of my favorites for many years. I am a door builder because I don't sit around and wait for opportunities to arise. They do arise though from time to time, and we need to be alert or we will miss them.

At this point on the agenda you are going to evaluate whether anything you thought about during the meeting could create some new opportunity,or could be hiding a threat. As you identify opportunities and threats you should compare them with your strengths and weaknesses. If an opportunity arises and you identify that you do not have a strength in that area,then it may not be a good opportunity to pursue. On the other hand, you may notice an opportunity that your strengths coincide with, and when this happens it's usually a good sign that it's an opportunity you might want to take advantage of. Of course, it also must be compared to your mission statement and vision statement make sure that is in alignment.

Chapter 7 Notes…

CHAPTER EIGHT

> *"Innovation is not the product of logical thought, although the result is tied to logical structure."*
>
> *Albert Einstein*

8 Agenda Item: Innovations

This portion of the agenda is my favorite. When done correctly, this should be the most fun, and should not be over-thought. This is the point in your meeting when you pull up and review any interesting articles about new innovations,or perhaps a brochure a vendor brought in about some new product you may want to carry. It can also be the time you would consider what you might want to do for your upcoming wedding anniversary that would be outside the box; for example, a walk on the beach where you discover a bottle washed up in the sand whichhas a personalized note for your spouse, followed by a quick lunch, or something else that would be fun.

This is really the time to allow your creativity to flow and to consider whether any of these new ideas would fit within your current set of goals. This particular step in the meeting should be something that you're planning for all week by saving ideas as they come across either electronically or in a file of some sort.

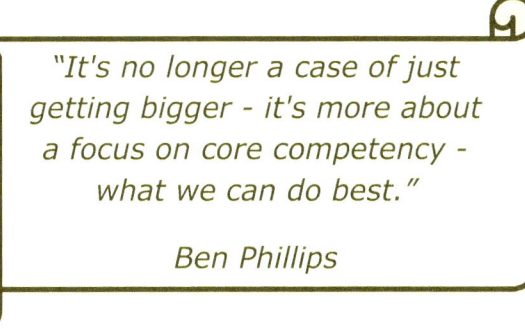

"It's no longer a case of just getting bigger - it's more about a focus on core competency - what we can do best."

Ben Phillips

It's not very often that a company does well with some new product line that is completely different than their normal set of core competencies. It does happen, but it's not something you should be setting a goal for. So, this portion of the agenda is where you look at any new innovative ideas and see if they fit the core competencies of your company, or your family, or your personal life. Knowing ahead of time that this is something you're going to do each meeting, you should automatically be looking for innovations that are at least somewhat related to your core competencies.

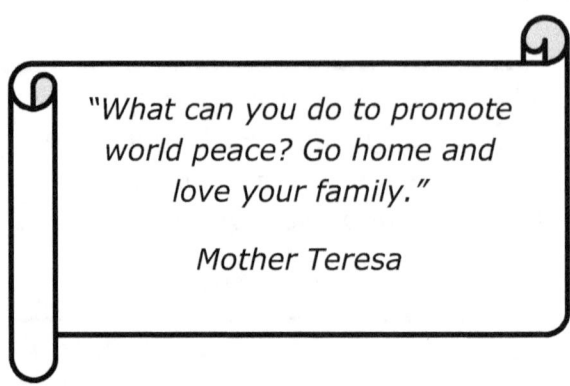

"What can you do to promote world peace? Go home and love your family."

Mother Teresa

This item on your agenda really has tobe personalized for you and your family. Suffice to say that this is where you will consider all kinds of outside-the-box ideas for yourself and your family, from new vacation ideas, to implementing a weekly game night, or involving children more in the decisions about meals or other activities.

If you decided that you wanted to start a special time chart with your family like we did,this would be a good time for you to brainstorm some ideas of thingsyou will do with your children during the upcoming week for special time.

This agenda item truly is individualized. You might be reading this right now and not even have any children and not be married. My ideas for this point in your meeting would not apply to you,unless you decided to run over to your brother's house and borrow their kids for special time. When you come up with some great ideas of your own, please make sure to visit our Facebook page and leave a comment about your personal or family innovative ideas. We can never have too many ideas to consider as options for improving our personal and family lives.

Chapter 8 Notes…

CHAPTER NINE

"Reduce your plan to writing. The moment you complete this, you will have definitely given concrete form to the intangible desire."

Napoleon Hill

9 Agenda Item: Action Plan

Now we get to the real work area of this meeting. On the sample agenda we set aside 20 min. for thissection. Some of the other sections may take you longer the first couple times that you hold a meeting because you're just getting used to the processes and knowing what to come prepared with. This part of the agenda should usually take the most time, because this is where you will formulate actual tasks and calendar items from the ideas that you considered earlier in the meeting.

Task Management& Execution

"The secret of getting ahead is getting started. The secret of getting started is breaking your complex overwhelming tasks into small manageable tasks, and then starting on the first one."

Mark Twain

It's also critical at this point to properly transition from your Saturday morning meeting into whatever format you regularly use to track your tasks and calendar items. Please don't forget about the idea that I shared earlier in the book about making a small square box next to task items or items that you need to take some kind of action on. Use that system right on your agenda, because it will make this step of the meeting a little smoother. You won't have to read through every note that you made in the previous sections. Instead, you can just scan the notes you took and look for empty checkboxes. Then you can transfer the items onto your task list or put them in your computer or smart phone, whichever you use as a method of organization.

Also, don't forget about reading the book *Getting Things Done*[14]. This book is filled with great ideas to become more organized with your tasks, and even teaches you how to process hard copies of documents and forms across your desk every day in a much more efficient way.

[14]Allen, D. (2001). Getting things done: the art of stress-free productivity. New York: Viking.

Chapter 9 Notes…

CHAPTER TEN

"True genius resides in the capacity for evaluation of uncertain, hazardous, and conflicting information."

Winston Churchill

10 Agenda Item: Evaluation

This portion of the meeting is kind of like the meeting after the meeting. It's an opportunity for you to review how the meeting went, and to assess your productivity during the meeting.

Take-Aways

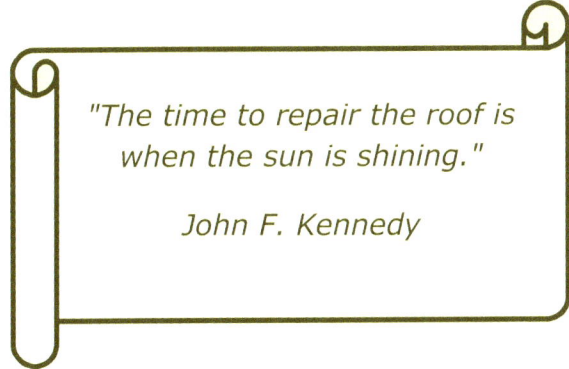

"The time to repair the roof is when the sun is shining."

John F. Kennedy

This quote by John F. Kennedy reminds me of being up on the rooftop with one of my boys while it was raining heavily, slathering on some gooey roof tar on the makeshift room that was really our back porch. Luckily, they make a product that you can apply while it's raining.

Of course, I did not pick this quote just to tell that story. This is an important part of the meeting because you're going to start to identify areas that maybe you didn't put enough emphasis on, or where you spent too much time. This is the point of the meeting where you put on the hat of the quality assurance manager and evaluate your performance during the meeting.

You should review how long the meeting actually took, and get a general idea of how long you spent on each agenda item. Just a quick review of how long it took will suffice. Also, you should identify how well you stuck with your alignment of personal and business mission and vision statements during the course of this meeting. Don't forget to take some notes in this section also. They will help you in future meetings as you try to uncover any areas that you might try to cheat and skim over in the future. We are usually our best own critics, and this is the time you should critique yourself.

Constraint Management

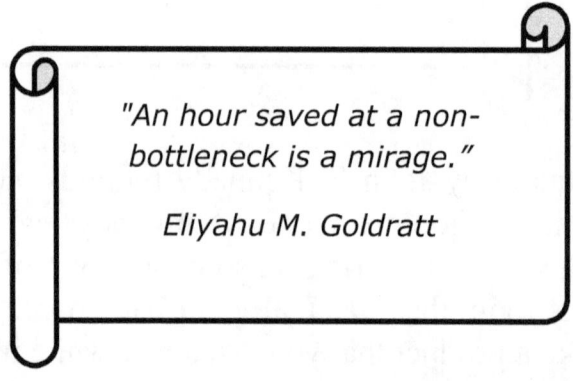

"An hour saved at a non-bottleneck is a mirage."

Eliyahu M. Goldratt

If you are the CEO of a manufacturing plant or major distribution center, then I would like to strongly recommend that you read the book *The Goal*[15]. The

---

[15]Goldratt, E. M., & Cox, J. (2004). The goal (Rev.ed. ed.). Great Barrington, MA: North River Press

quote above this paragraph is from the book, and it is one of the most enlightening and detail-oriented solutions-based books I have ever read. Every industry can gain some great information from the book, but it truly was written with manufacturing in mind. It is also the only business book I have ever read that had a storyline and character development. It is told as a story, so you grow to understand the struggles the plant manager was going through, and you feel like you're standing athis side as he discovers the solutions.

The primary theme of the book is constraint management. He discussed the need to study processes and uncover which part of the process isthe bottleneck holding up everything else from being producedat a more efficient rate. As you take a look at your performance during this meeting, be alert and aware of any potential downfalls that happened during the meeting. Was the location okay? Were there any distractions that could have been avoided? Was there a slow transition moving tasks and calendar items? As you review the meeting for a few minutes,have these things in mind, and always be looking for opportunities to improve them during future meetings.

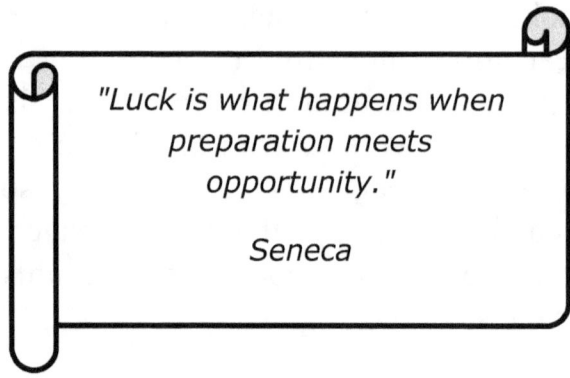

"Luck is what happens when
preparation meets
opportunity."

Seneca

Okay, this agenda item is simply the time that you will look and see what items need to be moved tothe agenda for the following week. Don't forget about the quick rating system. You can use either the ABC system or rate each item on a scale of 1 to 10. If you discover C items thatyou didn't have time to get to, those obviously go to next agenda. You also want to look for the checkboxes on items that might not fit into this week's schedule.

Chapter 10 Notes...

CHAPTER ELEVEN

"Tension is who you think you should be. Relaxation is who you are."

Chinese Proverb

11 Agenda Item: "Hammock Time"

The very last part of your meeting each week needs to be something relaxing that will also clear your mind to ready yourself for the rest the day. I really do have a hammock on the back to my property between two trees that I will take 15 min. or so just to lay down and relax and regroup. You should close your meeting in whatever manner you feel fits you, as we talked about earlier in the book.

Whatever you do, don't skip this part of the meeting. It's very important for you to really put your brain power into the meeting and then rest it when you're done. You don't need a hammock to take hammock time. Leisurely reading a book you might enjoy for 15 minutes after you finished the strategic planning meeting would be a great activity for hammock time. You may decide to take a walk afterwards or listens to music.

Do not use this time to watch the news. That will completely mess up the whole idea of hammock time. The news bombards your mind with information. It will not be something you remember as a pleasant experience after working so hard at planning for your upcoming week. Enjoy some time outside, or sit in the recliner and just relax without falling asleep. If you are a night owl and are having your Saturday morning strategic planning meeting on some other day of the week, late in the evening, then you might treat yourself to a little bowl of ice cream in that easy chair. Just try not to make excuses to have a planning meeting every day instead of every week just for some extra ice cream!

Chapter 11 Notes…

CHAPTER TWELVE

"To do more for the world than the world does for you - that is success."

Henry Ford (1863-1947)

12 Read This First

There is no mistake, this really is the title of the last chapter in the book. I chose this title for the chapter, not because I was thinking about putting it before chapter one. I really wanted it to stand out as something important. This chapter is the one I consider the ***most important*** of the entire book.

The first eleven chapters of this book were merely laying out a recipe for a way to become more productive, to increase your ability to balance business and personal priorities without having to take a month-long sabbatical to go "find yourself" first.

Some people will read this book with great goals set in their mind and hearts to conquer the world of industry, provide financial stability for their families for generations to come, or to get organized to start a new chapter in life. We discussed having passion in life's goals earlier in this book. Now I would like to take a moment to share something I have discovered during some of my formative years on this planet.

If you really want to tap into the deepest level of passion, the one with unlimited energies from a source that will never dry up, then serving others should be at the very top of your list in all areas of your life. Our perspective changes when we help others in life. We become more refined, and our senses are honed and tuned as we let go of selfish desires and replace them with an undying drive to help others.

I am not saying that we need to give up on our goals and dreams to move our family to Hawaii or take the whole family on a month long cruise (or whatever is on your list). Instead, I'm suggesting that we include as many service opportunities toward others that we can in our goal planning process and in our weekly meeting task creation process. You might be able to find opportunities to serve through your faith affiliation. You may also want to look into ways to serve in your community through a food bank, or helping children learn to read at your local library.

Compassion, love, and the joys that come from serving are stronger motivators than any brochure of the newest Lexus or yacht we might be interested in. Knowing that service has the strongest passionate power is the real secret to success in life. Without tapping into that power, people can still obtain fancy toys and buy the bigger home they want, but they will miss out on the true joy of success that comes from feeling the warmth of humankind that always accompanies passionate service toward others.

My wife, Cindy, and I have a desire to serve missions around the world with our church once our children have sufficiently locked into their adult pathways of life. Cindy and I have enjoyed the opportunity to serve as volunteer employment directors for our local church area, have served as teachers to adults and youth and have assisted with countless community service projects. I recently completed training to serve as a volunteer chaplain at our local hospital, and will begin that service this month. These service opportunities are the foundation to our joys and motivate us to achieve greater success. Higher revenue levels and financial security accompany success, but they are not where we should point our sails. When we open our sails into the winds of service, life becomes a truly joyous event full of challenges and blessings.

At the writing of this book, our son Michael is serving a two-year mission in the jungles of Peru around the Amazon river. We are so thankful that he can learn at the young age of 19 how strong the love is from others when we help serve them, and how powerfully it influences our lives as we continue to attain and set new goals.

As you become better focused through your Saturday morning meetings and experience greater success, your capacity to serve will be increased. If you keep this desire to serve highest on your priority list then you will see the greatest level of passionate energy become a regular companion in your walk in life.

Thanks for joining minds with me while reading this book. I have felt touched by everyone who will read this even as I am formulating the thoughts to put on these pages. I hope that these thoughts, ideas and suggestions have been helpful to you in your own journey in life. I'd love to hear your comments.

Chapter 12 Notes…

If you enjoyed sharing this time with me then I would really enjoy getting to know you better. Please feel welcome to listen in on Saturday mornings to our radio show, join our free announcement email list, become a regular recipient of the Saturday Morning CEO video tips, take an online class at the Saturday Morning Campus, join our Saturday Morning CEO mastermind family or at least come shake my hand at one of the Saturday Morning Boot Camps. You can find out all about these and more resources at www.SaturdayMorningCEO.com.

Saturday Morning CEO

Product and Services Discount Code

4942463

ABOUT THE AUTHOR

Many business authors are merely glorified journalists who interviewed many business owners and came up with their own perspective. Mr. Nurmela, on the other hand, is an author who has actually built companies from the ground up. He has experienced multimillion dollar business revenue success,and has learned from business challenges.

Denis began his first nonprofit business when he was nine years old. It was a neighborhood ecology club that did newspaper, aluminum, and glass bottle recycling. Even as a young man, when Denis served in the United States Air Force and worked many years as a surgical technician, he still maintained a part time business.

Mr. Nurmela founded and ran a variety of companies. One was an emergency alert software system that was designed for military recall, substitute teacher notifications, and public emergency related responses. Mr. Nurmela represented his company as a member of a congressional advisory board for the United States emergency alert system.

He was also founder and executive director of a human tissue surgical recovery service. This was not your typical business to begin as a startup. As you can imagine,it was highly regulated by state and federal agencies, including the FDA, OSHA, and was accredited by the American Association of Tissue Banks.

Denis and his wife Cindy have lived in the same small town in Southern California since 1987. They have raised six children, some of which have already started blessing them with grandchildren. They own just over 5 acres where they enjoy growing a garden, maintaining a small fruit orchard, and raise a variety of animals, including chickens that give them fresh eggs every day.

Mr. Nurmela is a sought after business consultant, coach, corporate trainer/speaker, and strategic planning meeting facilitator. He has also been a freelance business writer and a part-time college business professor. He oversees the Saturday morning CEO boot camp, video business tip subscription service, radio show, online training classes and mastermind groups, which can all be accessed at www.SaturdayMorningCEO.com

www.ingramcontent.com/pod-product-compliance
Lightning Source LLC
Chambersburg PA
CBHW051333170526
45166CB00002B/796